DEPRECIATING ASSETS

An Introduction

by W. T. Baxter, BCom, CA
Professor Emeritus of Accounting
London School of Economics

Published for
THE INSTITUTE OF CHARTERED
ACCOUNTANTS OF SCOTLAND
by
GEE & CO (PUBLISHERS) LIMITED
151 STRAND, LONDON WC2R 1JJ

FIRST PUBLISHED 1981
GEE & CO (PUBLISHERS) LIMITED

ISBN 0 85258 204 8

This study is published for the Research Advisory Committee of The Institute of Chartered Accountants of Scotland and does not necessarily represent the views either of the Research Advisory Committee or of the Council of the Institute.

Printed in Great Britain for Gee & Co (Publishers) Limited
by Cheney & Sons Ltd, Banbury, Oxon.

Foreword

This series of monographs has been initiated by the Research Advisory Committee of The Institute of Chartered Accountants of Scotland. The Committee believes that, at a time both of change and of increasing interest in accounting information, these monographs will meet a need for clear explanation of some of the more difficult concepts relevant to the preparation of corporate accounting reports. All are written by acknowledged experts in their respective fields in a style which will appeal equally to the specialist and the well informed general reader. Some will be relevant to the needs of one group more than to another, but they are addressed principally to accountants, bankers, civil servants, directors, financial journalists, investment managers, investment analysts, private investors, managers, trade union officials and others with an interest in accounting information. Opinions expressed by the authors are, of course, their own.

David Flint
Convener, Research Advisory Committee,
The Institute of Chartered Accountants of Scotland,
Edinburgh.

November 1980.

Contents

Preface

You will have noticed that depreciation often plays a big part in accounts. A balance sheet is likely to include machines, etc; it usually shows them at their cost when new, and then deducts the total depreciation that has been written off since their acquisition. And the income statement includes in its costs the current year's addition to that total.

Thus everyone who looks at accounts – investors, managers, bankers, students, and so on – should have some idea of how depreciation is calculated. What do the asset values and the costs mean? Depreciation measures can have a great effect on a company's results, yet they are chosen from a wide range of possible figures, by rules that are vague and little understood.

This monograph tries to explain the accountant's methods of dealing with depreciation and to suggest ways of testing these methods. But it is too short to cover all sides of its complex subject: you will have to read further to get a full view. You will gain much by so doing. For depreciation is beset by interesting problems, some of which are linked with lively controversies (*eg*, over inflation accounting). In what follows I must sometimes take sides in these controversies; however, when I do so, I try to point out that there are other views.

The monograph has five chapters. The first four sketch the framework, and attempt to establish logical rules for measuring depreciation in times when prices are stable. The fifth asks how these rules should be amended when prices change.

Earlier drafts have been read by the group that manages this series of publications for the Scottish Institute – Professors D. Flint and A.M. McCosh, Mr. P.N. McMonnies and Professor D.P. Tweedie; and also by Miss Winifred Elliott and Mrs Paula Walker. Their criticism was invaluable, and I am grateful.

W. T. Baxter
November 1980.

1 The Problem

Final accounts usually cover a year. So they would be easy to draft if the firm's happenings all came to a neat full-stop by the year-end – in particular if the firm could get all its inputs (goods and services) in doses that were used up exactly by then.

But a firm in fact buys inputs in doses that straddle business years: at the year-end its wealth thus includes sources of future inputs, such as stores not yet consumed, rent prepaid and machines that will still give service. The accountant must value these assets in his balance sheet. Likewise he must value the part of each asset that became input during the year and include this cost in the income statement. You will face the same problem if you keep monthly accounts, and have three-month season tickets or three-weekly haircuts.

The accountant's task may not be hard where the number of remaining input units can be checked physically and where the value per unit can be readily found. Thus stores-on-hand can be listed as so many tons or gallons, each worth so much money; and prepaid rent can be valued at so much per remaining month. Minerals (gravel-pits, oil-wells, etc) are less easy: experts may, or may not, know how many physical units are left; unit-values may or may not be well known and should presumably be trimmed to allow for, *eg*, increasing extraction costs as veins peter out.

Assets such as machines are a much worse problem. It is hard enough to define their invisible service-units, let alone estimate the residual number. And how do we find the value of each unit, especially if the asset will in future years grow less useful and need more repairs? It is mainly these difficulties that distinguish depreciating assets from the others.

Depreciating assets viewed as stores bought in bulk

Despite the greater difficulty of measuring and valuing the service-units of depreciating assets, the relevant principles seem much the same as for other sources of input such as stocks and stores. (And it should not matter, surely, that the balance sheet classes machines as "fixed assets" and stocks as "current".)

Our understanding of depreciation will in fact be greatly helped if we look on a depreciating asset in this light. We can imagine a firm that decides to buy stores (say, oil for heating) in bulk, because bulk-buying gives a lower unit-price and extra security and convenience. The oil is then consumed during more than one year; and accounting has evolved fairly adequate rules for charging each year with its usage and for valuing the residue at each year-end. Likewise the firm may choose to buy a machine with a long life because it is a better source of inputs, rather than buy a series of second-hand machines with shorter remaining lives or rent a machine by the month. The analogy with stores is thus close and should help us to devise rules for measuring depreciation.

The problem in diagram form

You may find that Diagrams 1 and 2 help you to see the problem. They illustrate the twin aspects of the asset's life-story: Diagram 1 traces its dwindling value over its life-span, *ie*, its value "pattern" or "profile"; Diagram 2 shows the fall in value during each year, *ie*, the yearly depreciation cost.

1. Asset value patterns

MC is the cost of acquiring the asset. KK′ is its final re-sale price ("salvage" or "scrap" value). MK is its life-span.

At the date of "birth", M, usually the only known figure is the price MC. The accountant can only guess how long the life MK will stretch and what the scrap proceeds KK′ will be (though past experience with like assets may help his guessing). And what sort of path does the value curve CK′ follow during the life?

The diagram suggests three of these possible value patterns between C and K′. They reflect three of the traditional accounting methods for writing off depreciation:

Diagram 1 **Asset Value Patterns**

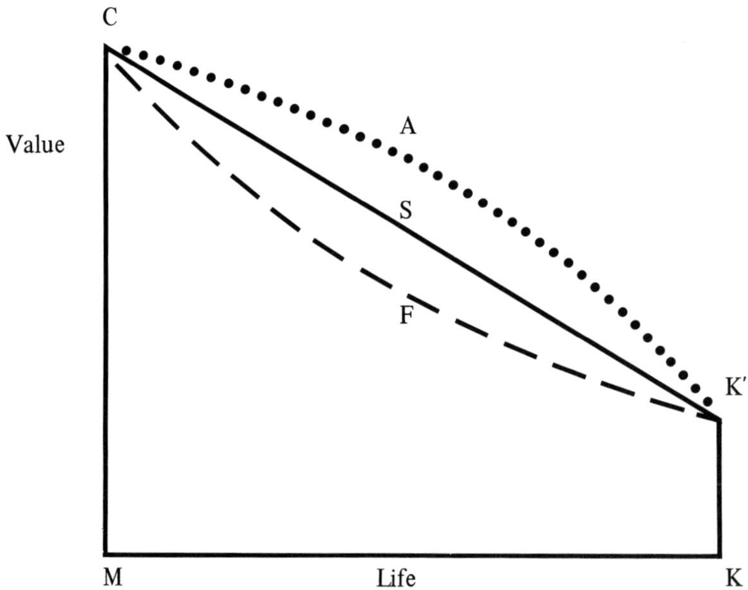

(1) CSK′ (unbroken line), found by *the straight line* method.

(2) CAK′ (dotted line), a "humped" curve, found by the *annuity* method (which allows for "interest" or "cost of capital").

(3) CFK′ (broken line) a "sagging" curve, found by the clumsily-named *fixed percentage of the diminishing balance* method. Most of the other popular methods also give sagging curves.[1]

The choice of curve can make a vast difference to the balance sheet figures, and to the value fall that must be written off each year.

2. *Yearly write-off patterns*

Diagram 2 shows three of the possible patterns of yearly write-offs (depreciation charges to successive income statements over the asset's life), namely

[1] The diagram suits an asset that, say, costs £1,300, lasts 16 years, and fetches £300 as scrap. The hump of CAK′ then accords with interest costs of 14% p.a. The fixed percentage here written off each year to produce CFK′ is about 8.75.

those reflecting the three value patterns of Diagram 1. (For clarity, the vertical scale of Diagram 2 is exaggerated.)

Diagram 2 **Yearly Depreciation Costs**

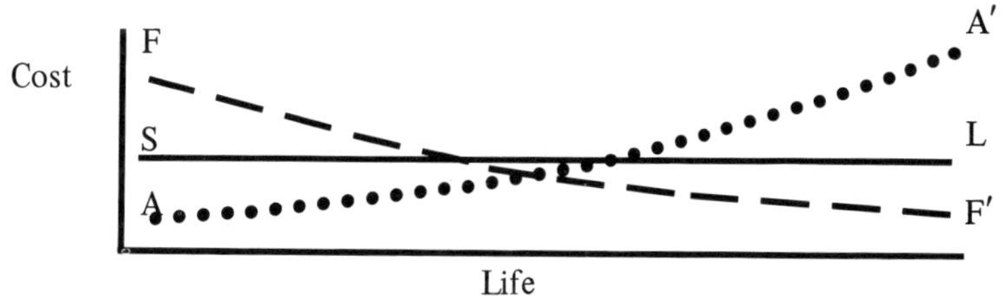

(1) The horizontal SL shows constant yearly costs (*ie*, the constant value falls of CSK′ above). It thus shows the depreciation charges of the straight-line method.

(2) The upward sloping AA′ shows costs that are low at the start but grow each year (*ie*, the increasing value falls of CAK′ above). It thus shows the net charges by the annuity method. This tilted pattern can be described as "low-high".

(3) The downward-sloping FF′ shows costs that are high at the start but shrink each year (*ie*, the diminishing value falls of CFK′ above). It thus shows the charges by the fixed percentage method. This pattern can be described as "high-low".

Our task is to ask ourselves which of the traditional book-keeping methods – the three illustrated above and some four others – best fits the circumstances of a given asset. And we may well ask, too, whether some quite different type of cost curve – say, one with much higher early charges – would not fit better; or whether we should not devise a special curve for each asset, instead of clinging to stereotypes.

Importance of using the best method

Even though the various methods all aim to write off the whole cost of an asset by the end of its life, the spread of this burden between years can be a matter of importance, particularly where depreciation is a big part of the firm's costs.

Profit figures are a useful guide to further investment. If the profits of a firm seem high, its owners will seek to expand it; and other firms will be attracted to the same field. Conversely, low figures discourage investment. Sound figures thus promote a healthy economy.

If then a firm chooses, say, a low-high depreciation pattern when a high-low one would suit the facts, the resulting tilt in the profit pattern will tend to attract too much investment at the start of life and too little at the end. The wrong choice of high-low rather than low-high may likewise distort investment in the opposite way. Thus the methods play a part in our economy's resource allocation.

They may also affect a manager's decisions. But here we must think carefully. Once machines have been bought, their cost must often become "fixed" in the sense that it is not varied by activity. Thus a manager should look very sceptically at decision-budgets that contain depreciation; usually cash flows are a far more reliable guide to true cost.

2 Concepts and Definitions

Value decline *versus* matching

Chapter 1's approach to depreciation (you will recall) takes decline in asset values as the base of its logic; its argument starts with change in successive balance sheets, not with costs in income statements. It is thus somewhat at odds with the reasoning often followed elsewhere which explains depreciation in terms of, for instance, "matching costs with revenues".

As the balance sheet and income statement interlock, the two lines of reasoning should lead in the end to the same conclusions. But the approach *via* assets is in my view both simpler and safer. "Matching" suggests mere ledger technique, not observation of economic facts. Its advocates tell us that cost must be distributed over the years "in a systematic and equitable manner"; but what do these fine words mean if they are divorced from decline in wealth? And surely assets can still depreciate even if there is *no* revenue to match (*eg*, where an activity has come to a standstill).

Current *versus* historical values

Note, too, that my argument may seem to imply freedom to use values found in the current market. In fact, of course, accountants mainly use historical costs (though the arguments for current figures now win mounting support – see the 1980 Accounting Standards (SSAP 16) on current cost accounting; depreciating assets are normally valued at some fraction of their original price (plus installation costs, et.), and the yearly depreciation charges are slices of this historical sum.

In my view, argument built on current values is clearer and more reliable than argument built on historical cost. Dead figures may not reflect today's realities; and they lack inherent logic. So current values are likely to point to the best depreciation methods.

But I do not think this conflict over theory need delay us. One can sensibly hold that methods found from current values, if adapted to historical data, will make the best of a bad job, *ie*, will yield the least indefensible historical measures. If this be true, the accountant should reason, when trying to choose a historical method, as if current and historical values will be identical, *ie*, he should assume that market values never change after the asset is bought. Here we shall start with this assumption (and so our discussion will help judgment of the historical methods); but later we shall relax it, and ask what should be done if assets are revalued to reflect current conditions.

Use-depreciation and time-depreciation

Some assets "die" when they are worn out by use. Others – perhaps most – die because of events that time brings anyway (regardless of use). For instance, machines may be scrapped because better models are invented; and a building lease runs out at a contracted date. It is thus convenient to talk of "use-assets" and "time assets".

The distinction is important when the accountant is picking a depreciation method. If the figures are to be helpful, a "cost" should be defined as sacrifice due to a given activity or event. So, with use-assets, a figure for depreciation cost should depend on extent of usage: it should be high in years of high use, low in years of low use. With time-assets, use costs nothing: value falls because the firm keeps the asset for another period; so the depreciation charges should here depend on passage of time. In other words, use-depreciation is a function of "service-units" such as miles run, whereas time-depreciation is a function of "time-units" such as the year.

Depreciation breeds "secondary assets"

Depreciation costs cut profit. Therefore, if owners take their income statement seriously, they will tend to pay out smaller dividends because of the depreciation entries. Then the firm will conserve cash. In time it may invest much of this cash (*eg*, in more stocks or even in other depreciating assets, or by repaying loan). Depreciation policy can thus help the firm to acquire a range of extra assets which in time improve the whole balance sheet. This helps to explain why it is economical for a new firm to start with few assets, and to expand later.

It is convenient to tack on the adjective "primary" to the depreciating asset whose pattern is our study, and "secondary" to the extra assets acquired thanks to the depreciation provisions.

Over the primary asset's life successive balance sheets will show a switch of values from primary to secondary. Thus, if a machine is bought for £1,200 at date 0, lasts for 3 years, and is written down by the straight-line method, the relevant bits of the balance sheets may run:

Table 1

Balance Sheets showing Primary and Secondary Assets

Date:	0	1	2	3
	£	£	£	£
Primary asset	1 200	1 200	1 200	1 200
Less Cumulative depreciation		400	800	1 200
Net value		800	400	–
Secondary assets:				
Bought with the year's depreciation quota		400	400	400
From earlier years			400	800
Cumulative		400	800	1 200
	1 200	1 200	1 200	1 200

This drift from primary to secondary can be illustrated also with diagrams. In Diagram 3, the vertical distance OC represents the owner's capital (= total assets), and OK shows the primary asset's life. CK – here, say, a straight line – traces the falling value. To maintain his capital despite this fall the owner must accumulate extra assets, shown by the triangle CC′K.

Depreciation policy can thus affect the growth and health of the whole asset structure. (Some critics ascribe the decrepit state of many industrial buildings in Britain to the fact that, until recently, British firms seldom wrote-down buildings.)

"Secondary earnings"

We now come to an important point that is usually missed. Though the balance sheet total may stay constant, the secondary assets swell the firm's

Diagram 3 **Depreciation and the asset structure**

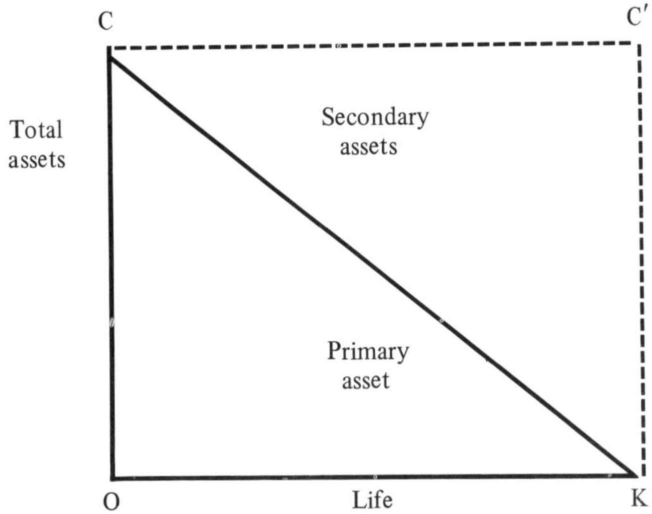

physical size. And, as the firm will not buy extra assets unless these yield benefits (more revenue or lower costs), total profit must tend to rise throughout the life of the primary asset. (In the Table 1 example, for instance, the £400 of secondary assets retained in year 1 will contribute to revenue in year 2). This is obvious where the secondary assets take the form of interest-bearing investments. These extra earnings, obtained thanks to the build-up of secondary assets, can conventionally be called "secondary earnings". They rise at a compound rate throughout the primary asset's life. When it dies, the cash outflow for its replacement tends to wipe out the secondary assets – and their earnings. The same cycle is repeated over the replacement's life.

Thus the preceding balance sheet and diagram, though good as a start to our studies, are rather naive – and so is much discussion of depreciation that ignores secondary assets and earnings. It is these that give the theoretical arguments for depreciation methods that allow for "interest".

Depreciation and replacement

You will sooner or later meet the view that the aim of depreciation policy is to save up the money needed to replace the asset after its death. Diagram 4 seems to lend colour to this view: the secondary assets KC′, particularly so far as they are liquid, must indeed be a help with replacement.

A corollary of this view is that, if we are to abandon historical cost and turn to inflation accounting, the right depreciation charge for any year must be a function of replacement price.

Many authorities back this idea. But it seems to me to be only a part truth. For one thing, it assumes that replacement will in fact take place. But suppose the owner plans *not* to replace the asset (because, for example, he makes supplies for North Seal oil rigs and will switch to other activities after the oil gives out). Does the asset no longer depreciate? The answer surely must be that it does – probably in the sense that each year sees the owner left with a smaller store of potential future services. Again, awkward problems arise where "Old" will be replaced by a very different "New" – say, one whose physical traits are radically changed or whose cost is far above (or below) KC′. At best, the replacement criterion is incomplete as a generalisation.

You must therefore ask yourself whether a better criterion is not *maintenance of the owner's capital* (OC in Diagram 4). Should not the test of depreciation policy be that it leaves the owner as well off (so far as the given asset is concerned) at the end of the asset's life as at the start? Here, of course, the difficulty is to define "well off". To my mind, the owner stays as "well off" only if his future receipts will enable him to maintain the same standard of living. During inflation, historical capital is certainly no guide to a realistic answer: the best guide is historical capital adjusted to allow for the fall in the £'s value (so that the best depreciation charge is historical cost raised with an index of general purchasing power). But here we are on contentious ground, and should postpone fuller discussion until we have covered the main framework.

Depreciation and tax on income

Page 9 pointed out that depreciation charges may lessen dividends, and so breed secondary assets. But that may also lessen tax, with similar beneficent effects for the firm.

The depreciation rates of tax law may differ from the rates that the firm deems best for its own accounts (which is one reason why taxable profit often differs from the profit in the firm's accounts). In his computation the inspector adds back the firm's figure and then deducts the official "capital allowances" instead. The official rules are far too complex for description here.

Governments often tamper with the tax rules in the hope of encouraging firms to invest more. In the mid-1970s business suffered from a liquidity crisis, probably aggravated by the failure of accounts to allow for inflation. The Labour Chancellor thereupon made new rules to ease the tax burden on firms hit by higher replacement costs of stocks and plant. The concession for depreciation is astonishingly generous: in many cases, the whole cost of a new asset can be charged in the first year. This allows effectively for inflation. But the two patterns of yearly charges (for tax and for accounts) are forced wide apart.

Obsolescence

This word has no very precise meaning, but we tend to use it when an asset's value falls for economic reasons that are not accompanied by physical decline. Thus a machine may be "as good as new" and yet lose some or all of its value because a better machine is invented or its products no longer sell well.

In accounts there is seldom point in distinguishing obsolescence from depreciation. At the start of a time-asset's life, when the accountant is deciding how fast to write it down, he tends to shorten his estimate of life if obsolescence is likely; then depreciation charges automatically include obsolescence cost. Only if value falls unexpectedly at some later date is a special obsolescence write-off needed.

Types of current value

Earlier paragraphs contrasted historical cost with "current value". These two words sound straightforward enough, but in fact they can mean several things, notably:

1. "Economic value" (EV)

We buy things because we rate them more highly than the cash that we pay as price. Thus, when a firm is deciding whether or not to buy a machine, it will – if it deems a sophisticated study worthwhile – draft a "capital budget" that sums the machine's benefits (perhaps wage savings and final scrap proceeds, less repair costs) all discounted to purchase date. These "discounted cash flows" (DCF) show the machine's economic value at the start of its life and can be compared with the purchase price.

(This use of the phrase "economic value" was popularised by the Sandilands Report.[1] You may well feel it to be unfortunate, since the other current values are just as "economic".)

2. "Market values"

(a) Replacement cost (RC)

This may be the current buying price. But sometimes other figures must also be allowed for. Thus, if I can replace an existing machine (call it Old) for £1,000, but an improved alternative model (call it New) will yield maintenance savings whose DCF is £200, the true replacement cost is only £800.

(b) Net realisable value (NRV).

This is selling price less any costs (such as agent's commission) still needed to effect the sale.

3. Deprival value (DV)

Since inflation accounting became topical, many British accountants have come to see that the most logical current value is *selective, ie,* found by choosing, according to the actual circumstances of each asset, one of the above three types of current value – EV, RC, NRV. This selective value[2] is sometimes called "value to the business" but that phrase seems vague, and (as the concept hinges on how much poorer the owner would be without the asset) I use "deprival value" instead. The "lower of cost or market" rule for current assets is a more familiar – but less rational – example of a selective value.

Deprival value is thus concerned with the worsening of cash flows that would follow the asset's loss. It can be defined as the lower of the asset's replacement cost and its expected direct contribution to cash flows. An undeprived owner will deal with the asset in the way that brings the highest contribution, either keeping or selling it; so "expected direct contribution"

[1] Report of the Inflation Accounting Committee, Cmnd 6225.

[2] The logic of such a value was first argued in J.C. Bonbright, *The Valuation of Property*, McGraw-Hill, New York, 1937, reprinted in 1965 by Michie Company, Charlottesville, Virginia. The first hundred pages or so of this classic should be compulsory reading for every young accountant.

(sometimes called "recoverable cost") means either economic value (*eg*, service in use) or net realisable value, whichever is bigger.

Thus the formula is:

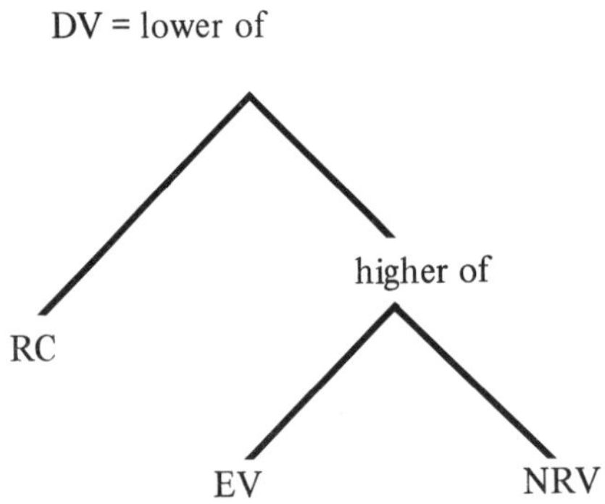

The reasoning behind the formula runs thus. Suppose a manager is deciding whether a proposed job is worth doing. His calculations must allow for the using-up of inputs (already owned), *eg*, stores issued for the job. To cost such stores, he must compare budgets of the future cash flows if he:

(*a*) uses up the stores on the job; or

(*b*) does not use them on the job, but retains them and then deals with them in the best remaining way.

The difference between (*a*) and (*b*) is the benefit of owning, that is, deprival value.

If he uses up the stores, normally he will replace them. Then budget (*a*) is at once burdened with their replacement cost; (*b*) is not; later cash flows are the same in both, as the replacements will yield the same contributions as the original stores and so these flows do not affect value. Thus, if the manager must buy replacements (for £70) because he will need such stores for a later job yielding £100, his budgets run:

	(*a*)	(*b*)
If stores are	*Used now*	*Not used now*
Then:		
cash outflow (replacement cost) is:	(70)	
cash inflow (future contribution) is:	100	100
	30	100

The £70 difference btween (*a*) and (*b*) is obviously due to replacement cost. This cost is here the deprival value of the stores; they are worth £70 to the business.

But sometimes the manager will not replace the stores, because *eg*, they have become dear or unsuitable. Then replacement cost drops out of the budgets. The difference between (*a*) and (*b*) is now the loss of the asset's future contribution – either NRV or EV; DV is the higher of these two.[1]

Current value patterns over whole life of a depreciating asset

For depreciating assets, the figures of each kind of current value will change as the asset grows older. Thus we must envisage a life series of, for instance, EV figures: the series starts high at acquisition date and sinks as the stock of services is consumed. Likewise NRV and RC values constitute series of diminishing figures.

Moreover "replacement cost" can mean two different sets of diminishing values:

(1) buying prices in the second-hand market (*eg*, a series of worn car prices, falling with age); and

(2) fractions of whatever cost the owner will in fact incur at replacement date. This series starts with, for example, the price of a brand-new car; subsequent values are geared to this initial cost. (Remember what page 4 said about viewing a machine as a store of inputs, bought in bulk at the cheapest rate per unit.)

So, when we are speaking of replacement values, clarity often demands that we add words to show exactly what we mean, *eg*, "replacement cost (new)"

1 I illustrate the budgets and give the reasoning more fully in chapter 12 of *Accounting Values and Inflation*, McGraw-Hill, London, 1975.

and "replacement cost in the second-hand market".

It is helpful to trace all the current values over the whole life of a depreciating asset:

Diagram 4 **Various value patterns of a depreciating asset**

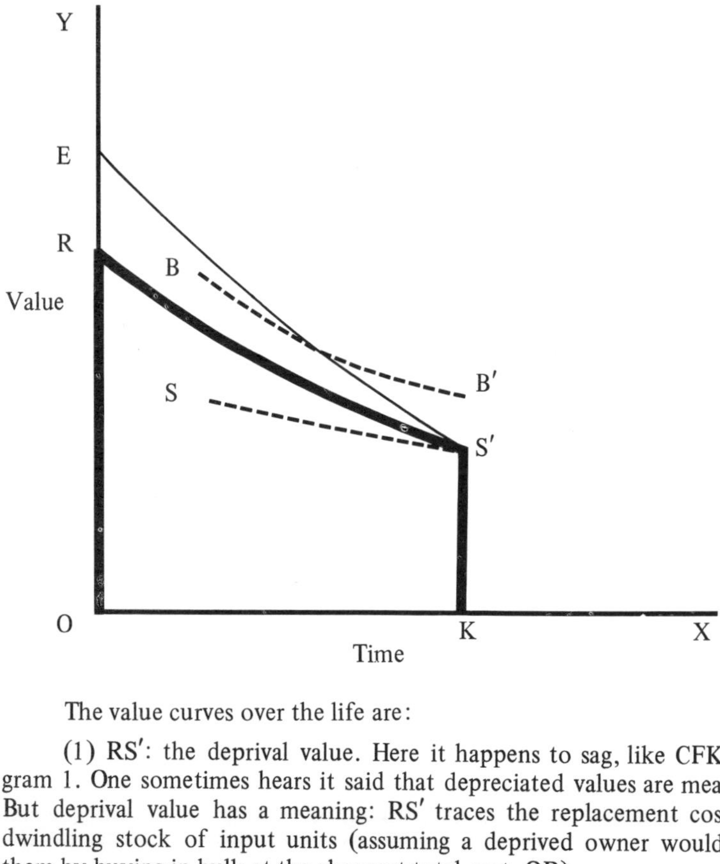

The value curves over the life are:

(1) RS′: the deprival value. Here it happens to sag, like CFK′ in Diagram 1. One sometimes hears it said that depreciated values are meaningless. But deprival value has a meaning: RS′ traces the replacement cost of the dwindling stock of input units (assuming a deprived owner would replace them by buying in bulk at the cheapest total cost, OR).

(2) BB″: the buying prices of similar worn assets (*ie*, replacement costs in the second-hand market). BB′ must lie above RS′, since the latter shows the cheapest source of inputs.

(3) SS′: the net realisable value of a similar worn asset. SS′ must lie below RS′ so long as the asset is worth keeping. Otherwise the owner would gain by selling – as he does at K, where KS′ is the scrap value.

(4) ES′: the DCF values of future services (plus scrap value KS′).

If you look back to page 15, you will see how its DV formula fits Diagram 4. Economic value ES′ is higher than sale value SS′ (otherwise the asset is not worth keeping), *ie*, ES′ shows the direct contribution; and so long as replacement cost RS′ is below contribution, it shows deprival value. At date K, both ES′ and RS′ are about to sink below SS′; sale price will soon be deprival value; the best plan is to sell the asset at once.

3 Choosing Optimum Life

Before he can decide on the depreciation charges for a newly acquired asset, the accountant must predict how long it will last (*ie*, the length of OK in our diagrams). Our textbooks are surprisingly reticent on how he does so.

"Life" is a matter of owner's choice

Unfortunately many kinds of assets do not "die" in a clear-cut way. Most assets have elastic lives: if the owner cares to spend more on repairs, new parts, etc, their life-spans can be stretched. Even where the asset is a living creature, its owner can often lengthen the span by spending more on diet and health care; when in the early nineteenth century the British navy cracked down on the slave trade, prices of American slaves rose – and they lived longer.

So an asset's life is best thought of in terms of the owner's cash flows. He is torn between two conflicting forces. On the one hand, he wants to put off replacement outlay by stretching the life. On the other, ageing assets suffer from various economic ailments – mounting repair costs, breakdowns, obsolescence, etc. The owner must try to find the best compromise between these forces, *ie*, the life-span that minimises his sacrifices.

Comparative budgets for various life-spans

He can find this compromise by putting the relevant cash flows into comparative budgets. Suppose for instance that the likely lives are in the range of 4 to 7 years. He must list the flows – initial price, repairs, etc, and scrap proceeds – for a life of 4 years, of 5 years, and so on.

But now he meets an unwelcome snag. He must not just compare, say, the 5-year total with the 4-year total (a process that would inevitably suggest the 4-year life to be the less costly). For, if he scraps Old at the end of year 4, normally he must at once pay for a New. To make comparison with the 5-year life, he must expand the budget of the 4-year life so that it not only includes Old's outlays in the years 0 – 4, but also allows somehow for the sacrifice of owning a New during year 5. Similarly all his other budgets must allow for overlapping lives.

The full solution is to extend his vision until it covers a very long series of 4-year lives, of 5-year lives, of 6-year lives, etc. This could be done by drafting a table of DCF budgets, embracing all years from now to his time horizon, to show which life-rhythm minimises the present value of future flows.

However, though logic demands this grandiose approach when conditions are complex (*eg*, if the costs of future News will change), happily there are ways of doing the calculations more simply if conditions are straightforward. The following example shows a crude but often sensible method.

Example

A firm buys a machine at year 0 for £130. The other cash flows for this type of asset are:

			£
Year	1 – 3	(no repairs, etc.)	–
	4	Repairs	10
	5	do	15
	6	do	25
	7	do	44

After year 7, repairs will be so high that a longer life is out of the question. Scrap value will be *nil* for all lives.

The optimum life can be found by drafting budgets (the vertical columns in Table 2) for each of the likely life-spans and then working out *the average cost per year* of each, as in the row marked C.

The lowest average cost is the £30 in the 6-year column; so the optimum life is 6 years.

Table 2

Comparative budgets to show optimum life

Year	4 £	5 £	6 £	7 £
A. *Old's cash flow in year*	10	15	25	44
B. *New's cumulative flows* over various potential life-spans:				
At purchase, year 0	130	130	130	130
In 1st, 2nd, & 3rd years	–	–	–	–
In 4th year	10	10	10	10
In 5th year		15	15	15
In 6th year			25	25
In 7th year				44
Totals for each life-span	140	155	180	224
C. *New's average* per year of life	35	31	30	32

Old dies when New becomes cheaper

It is important to understand the reasoning behind Table 2.

A firm scraps assets at the point of time when it benefits by doing so. Normally this means that Old is scrapped in the year when New becomes superior in terms of cash flows. The test, by this marginal approach, is that Old's pending flows for repairs, etc, will surpass a figure that measures – in constant yearly terms – the sacrifice of buying and maintaining New.

Averaging, as in row C, is a way of reducing New's cumulative flows to a constant annual figure. Thus the table's logic is as follows. Row A shows Old's remaining flows at any date. Rows B and C show New's flows, and point to their minimum average cost of £30. When Old's flows rise past £30, it should be scrapped. Columns 6 and 7, now A, show Old's flows rising from £25 to £44; so Old should give way to New soon after the end of year 6.

This simple arithmetic is defensible only where the first asset and its successor are expected to have the same flows (or perhaps where the future is so uncertain that the successor's flows just cannot be foreseen). If changed flows can be predicted for the successor, rows B and C must be altered accordingly.

Average yearly cost = notional rent

We should think twice before accepting the above average cost as a reliable figure.

There are cases in plenty where average (or "allocated") cost is meaningless or downright harmful. In the context of depreciation it can, however, correspond to a genuine economic quantity – a market price. An asset's services can be acquired by paying either one sum at the start (purchase) or a series of periodic sums (rental). The averages of our calculations are meaningful to the extent that they convert the totals of a purchase budget – such as a column in section B – into a constant yearly equivalent *ie*, a rent. So, to be realistic, the rent figure must suppose the lessor to bear the budget's repair costs, etc, and to receive the scrap proceeds; it would improve, too, if it were raised to allow for his interest costs.

Largely for tax reasons, many firms are nowadays tending to lease assets instead of buying them. So we are not being fanciful if we imagine an owner saying: "I shall scrap this asset when its upkeep grows to more than the rent of a replacement".

This analogy with rent can be useful over and over again when one is reasoning about depreciation. One may view the firm as if it were split into separate sections for (*a*) administration, and (*b*) operation. Then section (*a*) can be deemed to buy the asset and lease it to (*b*) at an imputed rent that just covers the net cash flows. This notional rent charge is an excellent guide when we are seeking for the right depreciation pattern.

Discounting

Many depreciation calculations can be made in either a crude or refined form. Refinement allows in particular for "cost-of-capital" or "interest". There are strong grounds in theory for such an approach: economic sophistication insists that £1 in year *n* is of less concern than £1 at an earlier date.

Accuracy must therefore fall if one relies on the crude form. Whether the error is big enough to worry about depends on the rate of interest and the length of the period.

It is reasonable to hold that the crude calculation of Table 2 is sufficiently accurate for the facts envisaged (especially as the data must in practice be subject to uncertainty). But a refined version[1] would tend to put optimum life at *more* than 6 years: and the higher the interest rate, the longer the life. "I use a high interest rate" is elegant for "I am hard-up"; and, for instance, the car owner who is hard-up (*ie*, short of ready cash, but perhaps wealthy otherwise) is apt to prefer costly repairs to the even higher cost of replacement.

Uncertainty

Figures such as those in Table 2 may suggest that the accountant can accurately foretell the future. Plainly that is not so. Most of his budgets are a kind of soothsaying. His firm may indeed be better off with such budgets than without them, but he must be ready for surprises and willing to revise his figures as time shows them to be wrong.

Optimum life budgets would seem particularly prone to error. Thus the Old in our example may turn out to be badly made, so that the repairs in fact rise faster than expected in the original row A, and bring death before year 6. Or, when year 6 comes, New's price may soar to a height that justifies extra years for Old.

Clearly, a firm with many similar assets can compile data that may lessen such uncertainties. You might suppose, too, that tables of asset lives (like the mortality tables of life insurance) would be available. But in fact they are hard to find. Even if such data existed, they would not help much (save where the firm owns enough similar assets to treat them as a group): if the actuaries' table for human lives put an age-group's average expectancy at *n* years, a given member may well die much sooner or later than *n*. In the same way, if tables of asset lives put the average at ten periods, individual lives will spread to either side. And in fact this spread seems to be remarkably wide. With some kinds of assets, less than 8% dutifully die in period 10; a few succumb in infancy, a few pass 20, and the majority lie scattered between these limits.

However, a study of depreciation (such as this) must for simplicity start by assuming the future to be predictable; otherwise it will get nowhere. And an accountant also, faced with a vast range of possibilities, is justified in working on this assumption when he picks a depreciation method. But surely he should later stand ready to modify his patterns if, as is probable, events give the lie to his first guesses.

[1] Shown in my book *Depreciation*, Sweet and Maxwell, London, 1971, p. 15.

The relevant cash flows for the comparative budgets

The phrase "relevant cash flows" crops up often in the above description of optimum life budgets. But by what tests do we decide which flows are relevant to those budgets – or indeed to any other budgets whose task is to aid decision?

The answer becomes clearer when we adopt the economist's "what difference does it make?" attitude. Let us suppose that we are deciding between two alternative lines of action, *X* and *Y*. We therefore draft a cash budget for *X* and another for *Y* to see which has the balance of advantage. These budgets should concern themselves only with flows that are a consequence of *X* and *Y*. Every flow (receipt or payment) caused by *X* should go into the *X* budget. Every flow caused by *Y* should go into the *Y* budget. But many of the firm's flows will occur no matter how it decides as between *X* and *Y*. These flows might go into both budgets; but then they would not affect the balance; and therefore logic as well as economy tell us to omit them completely.

Thus a flow is relevant only if it points the contrast between competing flows.

Where the decision concerns optimum life, in theory we contrast totals of future flows of rival series of say 4-year lives, 5-year lives, and so on. Differences between totals will depend on how often the replacement price will be paid and the scrap proceeds received; also on repair outlays of each year, so far as these change as the asset ages. These flows certainly are relevant.

With some assets, other flows are relevant too. Thus an asset may work less accurately in old age; the accountant should then try to put a cash value on, for example, the cost of its spoilt work. Again, age may sometimes lead to change in revenue; thus, if an elderly asset's breakdowns will cut output, the accountant must try to allow for the fall in receipts. One may, however, doubt whether the ordinary firm (with some spare capacity, and ability to get replacements fast) will let the aging of one asset have much effect on revenue; repair bills seem more likely to typify the ills of aging. We shall therefore in future pages tend to use the shorthand "repairs" for all the changes in an aging asset's yearly flows.

To illustrate. If the yearly wages of a repair team will be the same for this asset and its successor, they are irrelevant for optimum age budgets. But if the wages must rise because of aging, the increase is a relevant flow.

4 Patterns of Value and Cost

We now come to our central chapter. It looks critically at possible patterns of value and cost over the asset's whole life. It does so in four stages:

(A) This describes – in case you do not know them – the methods that accounting has traditionally used to write off depreciation. The methods are simple and convenient, but rough-and-ready. Different methods may yield very different costs. We must ask how the accountant should choose between them and, indeed, how far any of them reflect economic reality.

(B) This explains the patterns of deprival value for depreciating assets.

(C) This uses the patterns of deprival value to test traditional methods.

(D) This brings cost-of-capital into the discussion.

(A) THE TRADITIONAL METHODS

To set out the traditional formulae shortly, let us call the asset's original cost C, its scrap proceeds S, and its life n years.

In arithmetical examples let us say the asset's cost (C) is £1,250, and its scrap value (S) is £50 after a life (n) of 3 years.

The normal bookkeeping (illustrated below in the section on the straight-line method) uses three accounts. One is for the asset; it is debited with the asset's cost at the start of life and stays unchanged (unless the asset is revalued) till the final tidyings-up at death, The second, Cumulative Depreciation Account, is credited with the asset's depreciation charges year-by-year; its balance thus goes on growing till the end of the life, when its total is carried to the asset account. (The asset's value pattern is therefore the net balance of these two accounts). The third, Depreciation Cost, merely gathers together each year's charges for all depreciating assets as a preliminary to debiting total depreciation cost of the year to the income statement.

Straight-line

The yearly charge is $\frac{1}{n}(C–S)$ in all years.

In our example, it is thus $^1/_3$ (1250-50) = 400. The value pattern runs 1250, 850, 450, 50.

Diagram 5 **Straight-line method**

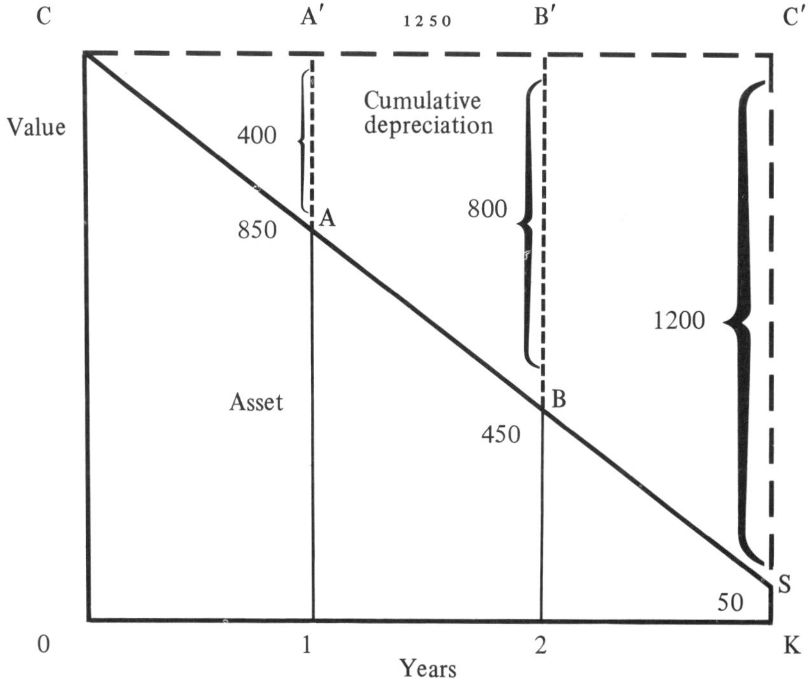

Diagram 5 may make the patterns more vivid. OCSK traces the (primary) asset's value. CC′S show how cumulative depreciation (= secondary assets) grows over the years – to AA′ (400), then BB′ (800), and finally SC′ (1200).

In the ledger, the same facts are shown thus:

Machine Account

		£			£
Year 0			*Year 3*		
Dec 31	Cash	1250	Dec 31	Cum. depreciation	1200
				Cash	50
		1250			1250

Cumulative Depreciation Account

		£			£
			Year 1		
			Dec 31	Depreciation cost	400
			Year 2		
			Dec 31	do	400
					800
Year 3			*Year 3*		
Dec 31	Machine	1200	Dec 31	do	400
		1200			1200

In practice, the scap proceeds are unlikely to be exactly £50, and so may prove too high or low to balance off the machine account. The difference is then taken to the current income statement (*eg*, if the proceeds are too low, the shortfall may be written off as extra depreciation of year 3).

Fixed percentage of the diminishing balance

Here the diminishing net value is each year written down by a constant percentage, so that the charges have a high-low pattern and the value curve sags.

In practice, some firms apply the method less primly than your textbooks suggest. They may for instance choose one plausible rate and apply it slapdash to a composite total value for many assets, with scant regard to whether these have similar lives or indeed still exist. Thus the method has been called "the lazy accountant's friend". Where he is not lazy, he must keep a separate account for each asset, and find the rate r – a fraction of 1 – from:

$$S = C(1-r)^n$$

or $$n \log(1-r) = \log S - \log C.$$

An awkward feature of these formulae is their sensitivity to the size of S – normally an uncertain and perhaps insignificant quantity. If S is small, and also if life is short, the first-year's write-off tends to be very big. Thus r is ·658 in our example and the write-off pattern is 822, 282, and 96. Value drops steeply (to only 428) in the first year: the extent of the drop can be seen by contrasting CABS in Diagram 6 with the (broken) line CS, showing the straight-line pattern.

Diagram 6 **Fixed percentage of diminishing balance**

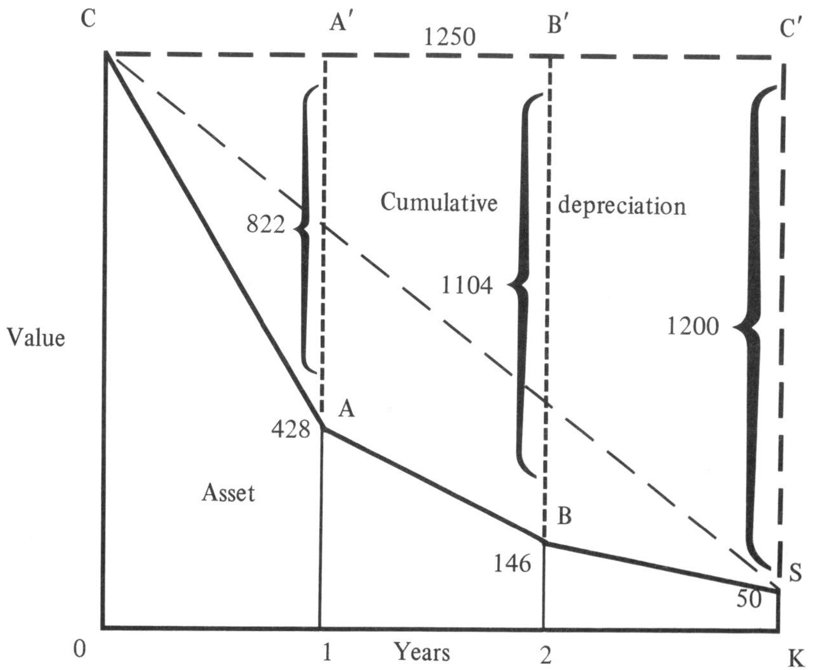

Sum-of-the-years'-digits

This method is popular in America. It, too, gives a sagging value curve; but the curve tends to be gentle and the arithmetic is fairly painless.

A decreasing fraction is applied each year. Its denominator is in all years the sum of the years' digits – in our example, 1+2+3 = 6. Its numerators are the digits in reverse order.

Thus, in our example, the fractions are:

Year 1 $\quad \dfrac{3}{1+2+3} = \dfrac{1}{2}$

Year 2 $\quad \dfrac{2}{1+2+3} = \dfrac{1}{3}$

Year 3 $\quad \dfrac{1}{1+2+3} = \dfrac{1}{6}$

The resulting charges are 600, 400, and 200. The book-values are 1250, 650, 250, 50. Diagram 7 traces these as the curve CABS - fairly near the straight-line values (broken line CS).

Double-declining balance

This, too, is used in America, to get a markedly sagging curve. The arithmetic is light-hearted: a fixed percentage is applied to the diminishing balance; this percentage is double that of the straight-line method where *S* is ignored. In our example, such a straight-line percentage would be $33^1/_3$; so the double-declining percentage is $66^2/_3$.

The resulting patterns are:

Year	*Opening value* £		*Rate*		*Write-off* £	*End value* £
1	1250	x	$66^2/_3$%	=	833	417
2	417	x	$66^2/_3$%	=	278	139
3	139	x	$66^2/_3$%	=	92	47
					1203	
Balance (roughly scrap value)					47	
					1250	

Diagram 7 **Sum-of-the-digits method**

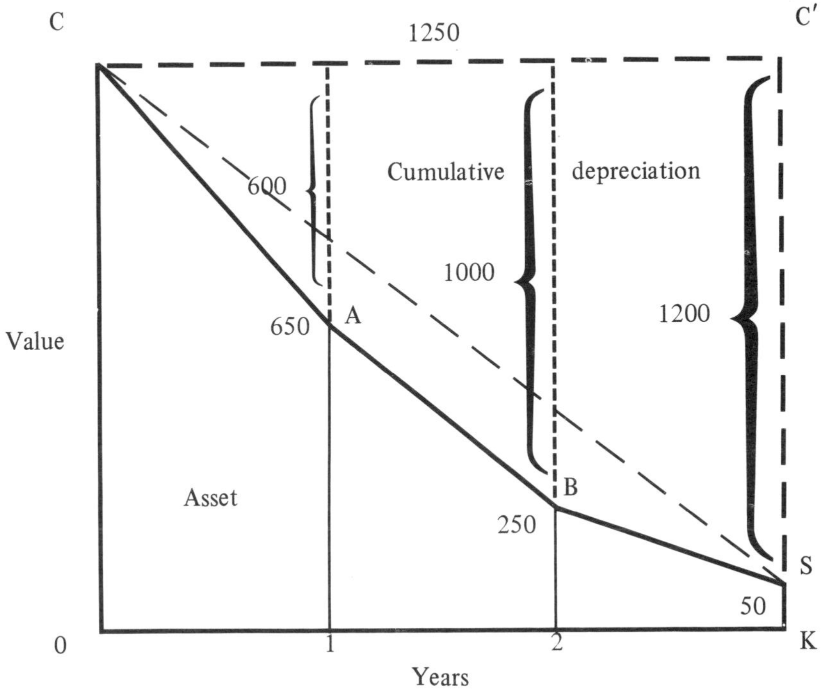

Fixed yearly charge to cover both depreciation and repairs

The above methods confine themselves to only two cash flows, *C* and *S*. It is arguable that we could with advantage widen their scope to include the flows for repairs.

The reasons are:

(1) Economic logic tells us that repairs – and sometimes certain other flows – are just as relevant to value calculations as *C* or *S*. Accounting treats the latter (as "capital" items) differently from repairs ("revenue" items); the distinction makes for easy book-keeping, but does not always have economic significance. Chapter II showed that repairs are part of the relevant flows for calculation of optimum life. Equally, they affect value. Suppose a firm has two middle-aged assets, A & B, identical save that B will need

costly repairs when it gets older; plainly this pending burden makes it less valuable than A.

(2) Methods that ignore repairs do not allow automatically for the asset's current state of repair. Suppose Asset C has just been given a major overhaul, whereas its twin D is in sore need of one; if the balance sheet shows both C and D at the same value, it gives a false view. Again, the income statement is open to criticism if it fails to allow for the high cost of pending repairs.

It is not hard to devise a formula that makes approximate allowance for repairs.

Let R = estimated total repairs during life. The yearly charge is then $\frac{1}{n}(C-S+R)$. This is a constant, and higher than straight-line charges; however, repair outlays are here not charged against profit but added to the asset's value.

Let us amplify our example by bringing in repairs of, say, £200 in year 2 and £400 in year 3. The yearly charge rises to $^1/_3$ (1250 – 50 + 200+400) = 600. The value pattern now runs:

Year	*Opening value*	*Write-off*	*Repairs capitalized*	*End value*
	£	£	£	£
1	1250	(600)	–	650
2	650	(600)	200	250
3	250	(600)	400	50

Diagram 8 shows this pattern. Realism and aesthetics both suggest that the £200 and £400 should be totals of smaller outlays, made every few months and growing as the asset ages. Then the value curve will be jagged, with teeth becoming more prominent over time. Moreover it sags below the straight-line pattern CS. It will always do so where the repairs increase with time.

Comparing Diagrams 7 and 8, one sees that both show the same values at the year-ends: 650, 250, 50. But in practice the two methods are likely to yield somewhat different values. To make them equal we have here chosen a repair pattern (0, 200, 400) that exactly complements the 600, 400, 200 depreciation pattern of the sum-of-the-digits method (*ie*, raises the total to 600 in each year). As later pages will explain, this choice of figures illustrates an important point.

Diagram 8 **Fixed charge to cover depreciation and repairs**

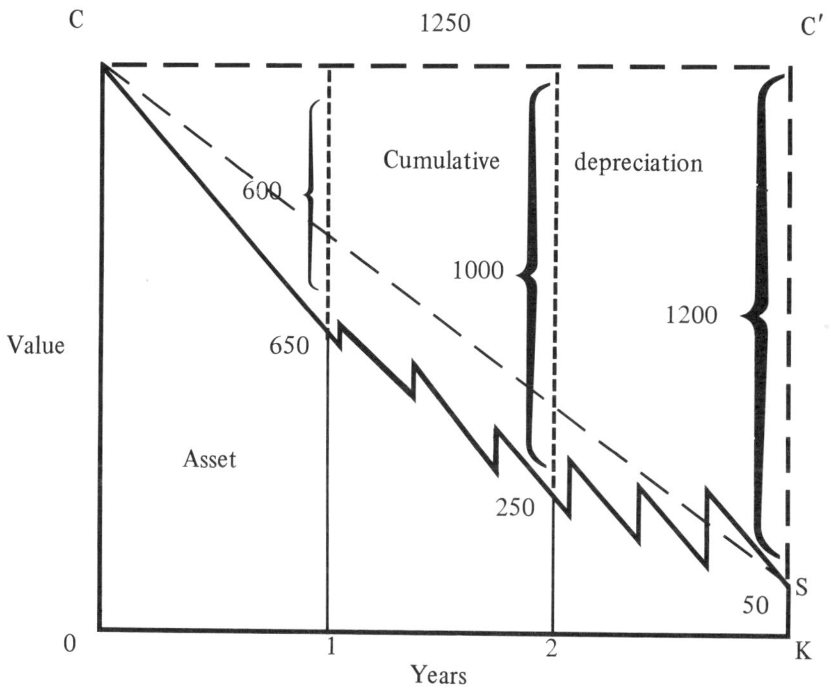

Service-unit

All the above methods are firmly linked to n, and thus assume that value drops because of time. They therefore seem suitable for time-assets. The service-unit method (and one or two slight variants, such as the depletion method for minerals) is linked instead to units that reflect activity, such as miles run or products made. It thus assumes the activity to cause the fall in value, and is suitable for use-assets.

In our example suppose the asset is expected to yield 100,000 service-units during its 3-year life. $(C–S) \div 100{,}000$ gives the unit-cost of £.012. The write-offs of each year depend on the service-units "consumed" during that year, say:

Year	*Service Units*		*Unit Cost* £		*Write-off* £	*End value* £
1	25,000	x	.012	=	300	950
2	60,000	x	.012	=	720	230
3	15,000	x	.012	=	180	50
					1200	

Here the asset is mainly used in year 2 and, accordingly, value drops sharply in that year.

(B) DEPRIVAL VALUE AND DEPRECIATION

Our next task is to find how depreciation is calculated when DV is guide.

The HAVE and HAVE NOT budgets

As page 14 explained, DV equals the decline in wealth that an owner would suffer if he were deprived of the asset. So DV is found by comparing his cash budgets for two alternative scenarios, namely if he (1) retains the asset (call this the HAVE budget); or (2) loses it (call this the HAVE NOT budget).

With depreciating assets the future flows are likely to be exceedingly complex, but we can reduce them to manageable size in two ways. First, we assume (at least at the start of our studies) that a deprived owner would buy a New, and a New with the same pattern of flows. Second, we rely on the idea that New's flows can be turned into a constant yearly equivalent (the notional rent of page 22 without violence to economic logic.

So the two budgets are likely to contain:

(1) HAVE

Old's flows over the rest of its life – namely "repairs" (in the broad sense that includes any flow changes due to aging), and final scrap proceeds.

(2) HAVE NOT

New's notional rent over the same period.

Note that the asset's contributions (cost savings or revenue) might not be lost at deprival; often New would yield them thereafter. Then they are common to both scenarios, and both budgets can omit them.

Layout of the budget

A convenient form for calculating DV (where this is as usual based on replacement cost) is a table with columns for each year of life, and rows for:

i. Old's cash flows (the HAVE budget).
ii. New's cash flows, converted into a constant notional rent (the HAVE NOT budget). Where New's flows are the same as Old's, the rent is the average of the figures in row *i*.
iii. The excess of *ii* over *i*, i.e. the net benefit of ownership during each year.
iv. The total net benefits still to be received at each year-end, i.e. the sum of the *iii* figures in the columns further to the right.

Thus *iv* gives the DVs (the replacement costs of remaining input units) for consecutive balance sheets, and *iii* gives each year's write-off.

Example

Let us put the *C* and *S* of our staple example into such a table. It then looks like this:

Table 3 *Deprival value of a depreciating asset (no repairs, etc.)*

Year of Life		0	1	2	3	3′
		£	£	£	£	£
i HAVE budget						
Old's cash outflow		1250				
Old's cash inflow						(50)
	£					
Net total	1200					
average p.a.	400					
ii HAVE NOT budget						
New's notional rent			400	400	400	
iii Benefit of owning for year (*ie* write-off at year end)			400	400	400	50
iv Deprival value (= future years' benefits per *iii*)		1250	850	450	50	-

(C) TESTING THE TRADITIONAL METHODS

Straight-line

The figures in rows *iii* and *iv* of Table 3 turn out to be the very same as those of page 26, illustrating the straight-line method. Thus the DV approach triumphantly confirms that this popular method has validity – always provided actual conditions match Table 3's assumptions, namely:

(1) the asset is a time-asset; and

(2) repairs (and other yearly flows) are constant over life; and

(3) cost-of-capital can be ignored; and

(4) all prices are constant.

Sagging curves

Where, instead, the flows get worse over the years, DV no longer sinks in a straight line.

Suppose again there are repairs of £200 in year 2, and £400 in year 3. Now the budgets change to the figures of Table 4, page 36.

Here the write-offs follow a high-low pattern; the value curve drops steeply at first and gently later. So a traditional method that produces a sagging curve may meet our needs.

In fact, because we have here used repair figures (0, 200, 400) that complement the write-offs of our sum-of-the-digits example (page 29), the two sets of values are the same. Given this repair pattern, the sum-of-the digits method is a short-cut to DV values. With other repair patterns, it might not be so suitable; the fixed-percentage methods might (or might not) fit better.

Fixed charge for depreciation and repairs

DV'S yearly write-offs, as shown in row *iii* of Table 4, complement each year's repairs, etc. to produce a constant total charge for the two costs. This is logical where the repairs are debited to the income statement as

Table 4

Deprival value of a depreciating asset (with repairs)

Year of life	0	1	2	3	3′
	£	£	£	£	£
i HAVE budget					
Old's cash outflows	1250		200	400	
Old's cash inflow					(50)
£					
Net total 1800					
Average p.a. 600					
ii HAVE NOT budget					
New's notional rent		600	600	600	
iii Net benefit of owning for year (*i.e.* write-off at year-end)		600	400	200	50
iv Deprival value (= future years' benefits per *iii*)	1250	650	250	50	-

a separate item (the usual bookkeeping). But, particularly where repairs are pending at the year-end, a still better course would be to debit the full rent of row *ii* to the income statement, and the repair outlays to the enlarged cumulative depreciation allowance.

But this is precisely what the fixed-charge-for-depreciation-and-repairs method does; the diagram that illustrates it (page 31) could equally well be used for Table 4's DV figures. So this method wins high marks by the DV test. Unfortunately it is less popular than the other methods, presumably because the unpredictability of repairs lessens the chance of neat end-figures at the asset's demise.

Service-unit methods

Obviously any "consumption" of a use-asset during a year must lessen the owner's loss if he is deprived at the year-end. Therefore DV must respond to such consumption.

DV figures for a use-asset can be found by changing the rents in row *ii* of the tables: instead of the constant for each year, we put in a charge per use-unit, multiplied by the year's number of units. Given the facts assumed by the example on page 32, the DV values will be the same as those of that example.

However, a more realistic example would include repairs also. DV tables would here end with more sensitive values, influenced by both use and repairs. This suggests that accounting should combine two methods, *ie*, service-unit and fixed-charge-for-depreciation-and-repairs.

Summary

To re-cap. By recording declines in asset value, accounts create charges in income statements. These charges should represent a constant cost per unit of fixed asset "consumed" by use or passage of time (*cf*. charges for stores). A depreciation method meets this test if it charges the income statement with either:

(1) a cost that complements other relevant flows charged in the given year, so ensuring a constant total charge per unit; or

(2) a constant cost that is high enough to cover not only conventional depreciation but also the other relevant flows, which must here be capitalised.

With such a method, asset values become sensitive to the remedial effects of overhaul, etc, and then may have a somewhat saw-like pattern.

Where a traditional method comes close to meeting this test, then its use is justified. Where none of the traditional methods answer, then surely the accountant should devise a special method, with the help of DV analysis.

(D) INTEREST

Asset value can be approached in two different ways (which, under ideal conditions, yield the same figure): (1) forward-looking; and (2) backward-looking. Thus, to find a mid-life value of a depreciating asset we can either (1) look back to original cost and other relevant past flows, and write off depreciation; or (2) look forward to future flows, as in a table of HAVE and HAVE NOT budgets.

Both methods grow in accuracy if they allow for interest. In (1), interest on the investment is as truly a cost as outlays on *eg*, installation or foundations. In (2), discounting makes for realism (indeed, long-range calculation becomes senseless without it): capital budgets and DV budgets both gain if they treat the firm's cost-of-capital as an ingredient.

Thus it seems sad that we make so little use of methods that allow for interest. There are plenty of reasons for our neglect, such as: (1) the methods are not simple; (2) interest cost on a given asset is inconspicuous – a concealed part of the firm's total cost-of-capital (which itself is apt to be inconspicuous); (3) humped value curves seem at odds with conservatism; (4) accountants are bad at compound interest.

Methods that allow for interest

Our textbooks usually extend their list of traditional methods by adding the annuity method and the sinking fund method. The distinction between these two seems to relate less to principle than to type of secondary assets (with sinking funds, usually external investments such as government stocks).

It is, however, helpful to regard an "interest method" not as an addition to the usual list but rather as an improved version of a method that ignores interest. Thus the straight-line method burgeons into the annuity method when interest is recognised. And all other methods could likewise, with a little ingenuity, be spruced up to allow for interest.

Annuity method

The "annuity" in question is in fact DV's notional rent series, increased by interest. Suppose the only cash flow of an asset with a 3-year life is its price of £1,000, and the firm's cost-of-capital rate is 10%. Interest tables show that, at 10%, 2.487 buys a 3-year annuity of 1; therefore 1,000 buys one of 1000 ÷ 2.487 = 402. The latter figure is the annual charge by the annuity method.

The cash flow of our usual example includes the £50 received in year 3. To find the yearly rent, *U*, we must allow not only for the price of £1250 but also for present value of £50. If the cost-of-capital rate is 10%, then tables put the present value of 1 due in 3 years at .751, and U is found from:

$$1250 = 2.487\,U + 50 \times .751$$
$$\therefore U = 487.54$$

Backward-looking approach

The easiest way to show the method's mechanics is *via* the backward-looking approach of the historical cost ledger, with one combined account for the asset and depreciation. Each year this account is debited with interest on the opening balance, *ie*, the depreciated value is raised by this cost; the credit is put into (say) the finance section of the income statement, probably as an offset to interest paid. The asset account is credited with the full depreciation charge; the debit goes eventually to the income statement, *eg*, as a manufacturing cost.

An example of the asset account follows:

Machine account

	£		£
Year 1		*Year 1*	
Jan. Cash	1250.00	Dec. Manufacturing a/c	
Dec. Interest	125.00	(depreciation charge)	487.54
		Balance c/d	887.46
	1,375.00		1,375.00
Year 2		*Year 2*	
Jan. Balance b/d	887.46	Dec. Manufacturing a/c	
Dec. Interest	88.75	(depreciation charge)	487.54
		Balance c/d	488.67
	976.21		976.21
Year 3		*Year 3*	
Jan. Balance b/d	488.67	Dec. Manufacturing a/c	
Dec. Interest	48.87	(depreciation charge)	487.54
		Cash	50.00
	537.54		537.54

Forward-looking approach

The forward-looking approach of DV budgets yields the same values. The HAVE budget must include interest as a cost, and the HAVE NOT budget must use the high rent of £487.54 (which, adopting the actuaries' wording in loan repayment tables, can be called the "full service charge"). Table 5 shows the calculation:

Table 5

Deprival value of a depreciating asset (interest recognised)

Year of life	0	1	2	3	3′
	£	£	£	£	£
i HAVE budget					
Old's price	1250				
Interest on balance per *iv*		125	88.75	48.87	
Scrap proceeds					(50)
ii HAVE NOT budget					
New's full service charge		487.54	487.54	487.54	
iii Benefit of owning for year (*ie*, net write-off at year-end)		362.54	398.79	438.67	50
iv Deprival value (=Future years' benefits per *iii*)	1250	887.46	488.67	50	

These values follow a humped course (somewhat like CAK′ in the diagram on page 5).

Where the HAVE budget includes rising repairs, these will tend to offset interest's effect on the value pattern: sagging force now conflicts with humping force. The resulting pattern may approximate to a straight line. Perhaps this is a justification for use of the straight-line method.

Final accounts for each year of life

A table of final accounts, covering the whole life, gives satisfying proof of the annuity method's logic.

Suppose that the asset in our example earns about £738 a year (after all the costs except depreciation) throughout its life; that secondary assets earn 10% and that the owner withdraws all profit. Table 6 shows the full story.

Table 6

Annuity method in a complete set of final accounts, over whole life

Year	1	2	3
	£	£	£
Balance sheet			
Primary asset			
Balance brought forward	1250	887	488
Add 10% cost-of-capital	125	89	49
	1375	976	537
Less Depreciation	488	488	487
Net value	887	488	50
Secondary assets	363	762	1200
Total (= capital)	1250	1250	1250
Income statement			
Operations			
Revenue	738	738	737
Less depreciation	488	488	487
	250	250	250
General			
Secondary earnings		36	76
Cost-of-capital added to primary asset	125	89	49
Total	125	125	125
Total profit (= dividend)	375	375	375
Rate of return on £1250 investment	30%	30%	30%
N.B. Depreciation can be analysed as:	£	£	£
Net value write-off	363	399	438
Cost-of-capital	125	89	49
Full service charge	488	488	487

The humping produced by interest can be seen by comparing the pattern of net values (887, 488, 50) with the straight-line values (800, 400, 50).

Note the following:

(1) We must be careful to distinguish between *gross* and *net* depreciation (see analysis at the foot of the table). The gross (= full service) charge is constant over the years. But, because high-low interest costs are added to the asset balances, the net write-offs are less than the full charge, and are tilted low-high.

(2) Thus net charges against revenue rise each year. But so do secondary earnings – to exactly the same extent, thanks to our use of the secondary earnings rate of 10% in the calculation of the charges.

(3) Therefore profit is constant over the 3 years – and also over later 3-year cycles if these are repeated. The rate of return on the £1250 investment (30%) is constant too. These constant figures seem the best guide to users of the accounts, given our assumption of stable revenue, etc. If you re-write the table with a method that ignores interest, you will get tilted figures.

Full and net cost curves

Diagram 9 shows the various cost curves that result from recognition of interest. AA′ traces the full service charge, *ie*, the constant gross figure. DD′ traces the net charge. The vertical distance in any year between these curves represents the cost-of-capital.

For comparison, the diagram shows too the straight-line charges, SL. The positions of the other curves imply a high rate of cost-of-capital and a long life; otherwise these curves would lie closer to SL.

The full service charge would seem a useful tool for management control. Because it includes imputed interest, it is better than, say, the straight-line method for showing the whole sacrifice caused by asset ownership. Manufacturing accounts with such high charges would tell everyone how much the works manager's equipment really costs the firm, and perhaps make him more cautious in his requests for fresh investment.

Diagram 9 **Net and gross charges where interest is recognised**

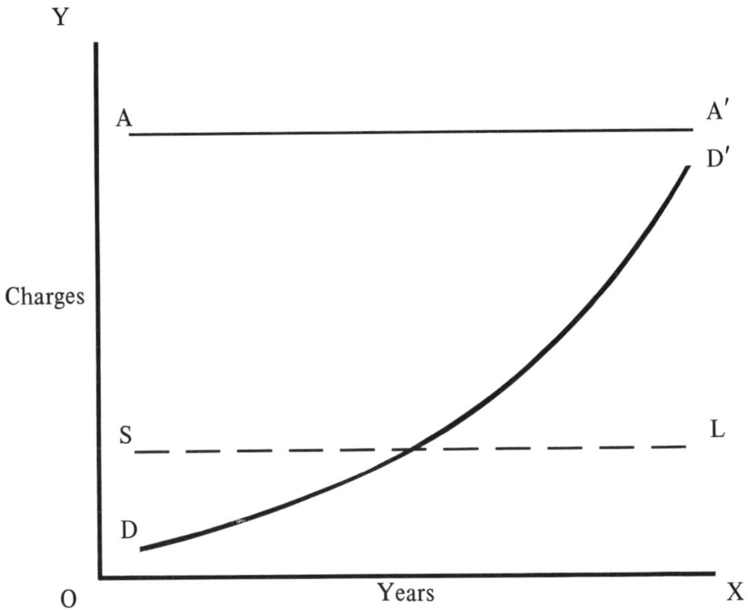

5 *Revaluation*

Up to this point we have for simplicity assumed that prices, etc, remain stable. We must now abandon this assumption, and deal with changing conditions and their effects on value patterns.

So long as accounting uses historical costs, changing conditions will affect its value patterns to only a very limited extent (as where obsolescence causes a faster write-off).

If, however, a firm relaxes its adherence to historical cost, revaluation may often be necessary. Then the attitude and techniques of deprival value become exceedingly helpful. Tables of HAVE and HAVE NOT budgets, such as that on page 36, again meet our needs; but they must be amended, at the date of change, to make their later figures match the new conditions. In particular, New's notional rent must be updated. Then the revised depreciation and value patterns emerge automatically.

We can best deal with our topic under the heads of (*A*) general price-change (since 1939, inflation); (*B*) price-change specific to the given asset; and (*C*) combination of both general and specific change. Understanding is easier if we suppose the change to be abrupt, *ie*, confined to one year; and if we overlook the refinement of discounting.

(A) INFLATION

Common sense suggests that, if the general index goes up by, say, 40% , revaluation must lift the historical cost patterns of later times by 40% too. But common sense is right only if the price-change is indeed general, affecting *all* the relevant flows to an equal degree.

Asset values

Suppose, in the example on page 36, that the 40% rise occurs at the end of year 2 (and after the £200 repair of that year). If we do a formal calculation, we must redraft Table 4, splitting its year-2 column into pre-change and post-change parts. Table 7 is the result. After the rise, all the figures go up by 40%, *eg*, New's rent jumps to £840.

Table 7

Revaluation after inflation

Year of life	*0*	*1*	*2* *Pre-*	*Post-*	*3*	*3*
	£	£	£	£	£	£
i HAVE budget Old's Cash flows	1250		200		560	(70)
ii HAVE NOT budget New's notional rent		600	600		840	
iii Net benefit of owning for year		600	400		280	70
iv Deprival value – future years' benefits, as foreseen:						
Prior to inflation (line *iii*, page 36)	1250	650	250			
After inflation (per *iii* above)				350	70	

Thus row *iv* confirms what one would expect: value rises 40% at the time of price-change – from £250 to £350.

Diagram 10 illustrates the change of pattern. It assumes repair costs (*eg*, the £200 of year 2) to consist of many small payments, so that we are justified in smoothing the value curve. Over the whole life, value follows the pattern CFHSK, instead of the original prediction of CFK′.

It is important to recognise how limited is inflation's impact on these patterns. (It can elsewhere have great effect, *eg*, by reducing the purchasing power of cash and other assets whose values are tied to the £.) All that our calculations do is to re-state the post-change facts in a money-unit of lower worth, much as if the ledger was switched from £s to $s. The facts themselves

Diagram 10 **Asset revaluation because of inflation**

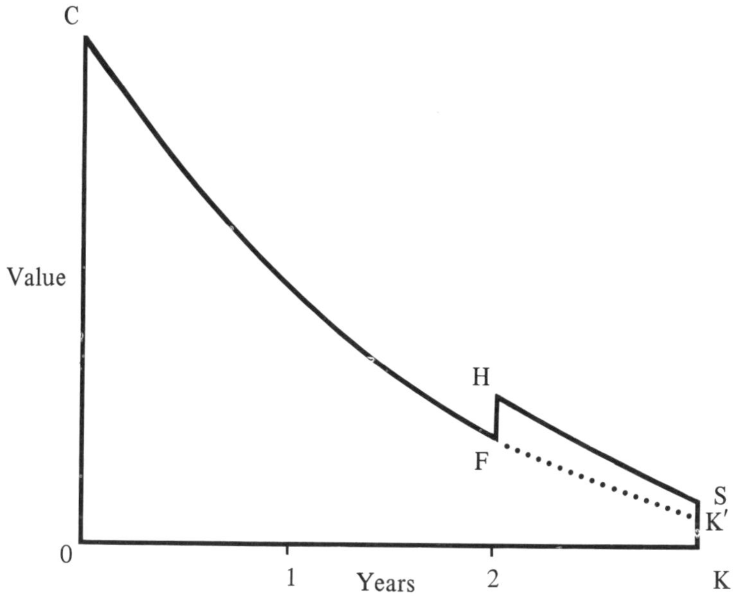

do not change; for instance, an optimum life table for New (on the lines of the table on page 21) would show that New's life neither grows nor shrinks. If the vertical axis of Diagram 10 measured value in units of constant purchasing power, the value curve would retain its original pattern.

The revised balance sheet

If the revised net value of the depreciating asset is to go into the balance sheet, other figures must change also. To be consistent with the normal layout, we must show the asset's gross value and cumulative depreciation; so, in our example, both of these must be raised by 40%. The secondary assets will presumably be revalued also (so far as they are not monetary items). The equity must then go up, to maintain balance: theory bids us raise the capital, but in fact the needed increase is likely to be shown separately, with some such name as "inflation allowance".

For our page 45 example, the balance sheet at the end of year 2 must thus be revamped as in Table 8.

Table 8

Balance sheet, end of year 2, revalued after inflation

	(1) *Pre-revaluation*	(2) *Post-revaluation*
	£	£
Primary asset (cost, new)	1250	1750
less Cumulative depreciation	1000	1400
Net value (worn)	250	350
Secondary assets	1000	1400
	1250	1750
Capital	1250	1250
– inflation allowance:		
primary asset		100
secondary assets		400
		500
	1250	1750

Annual charges

In the years after the price rise, the annual write-offs should, if the owner is to maintain his real capital, be higher than historical cost charges – *ie*, should be the historical figures raised with a general index factor. Revaluation yields these higher figures automatically. In our example, the year 3 charge is put up by 40% and becomes £280 instead of £200; and so the owner will end up with his real capital unimpaired (*ie*, with 1750 of the end-£s, equivalent in his eyes to 1250 of the beginning-£s).

The backlog bogie

Some people argue that, after each price change, the next income statement must be charged not only with a revised depreciation cost of the current year, but also with "backlog" depreciation to boost the contributions of earlier years. Thus, in the example, they would have us charge an extra £400 to top up the historical depreciation of column (1) from £1,000 to £1,400.

This is yet another instance of how historical figures can confuse. If the balance sheet is corrected to current £s, it shows that inflation in fact brings no need for backlog charges: in column (2) depreciation is re-stated at the proper figure of £1,400 without any boosting. And, if there is further inflation in future years, depreciation will go on rising automatically in corrected accounts.

But, you may argue, the post-revaluation figures of Table 8 are so healthy only because the secondary assets appreciate there by 40%; and they will fail to do so if they include net monetary assets (since the face value of such assets does not change). True: but then the failure is due to liquidity policy, not depreciation; the accounts mislead if they blame the shortfall on "backlog depreciation" instead of "loss on holding money".

(B) SPECIFIC PRICE CHANGE

In this section, we assume one or more of the relevant flows to change during a period when general prices remain tolerably constant. So here we are dealing with *relative* change – something that is likely to have economic consequences of importance; any rise or fall in value is now "real", as distinct from the "nominal" or "fictitious" movements of inflation.

Revised figure of optimum life

Let us suppose that the 40% rise in our example is confined to New's price (*ie*, repairs and scrap value stay unchanged). This shift makes replacement more disagreeable, and so tends to lengthen life (put at 3 years on earlier pages). To find what happens, we must look at the flows of years 4 and 5; let us say the repairs will be £700 in 4 and £1300 in 5. The optimum life calculation (explained on page 20) becomes (see Table 9; page 49).

Thus New's optimum life rises to 4 years (instead of 3), and its notional rent to £750 (instead of the £600 on page 36). What about Old's life? If Old is kept during year 4, its net flow will then be £700 less scrap £50, *ie*, £650 – less than New's rent. If Old is kept during year 5, its net flow will be £1,300 less £50, *ie*, £1,250 – more than New's rent. So Old should now be kept till the end of year 4 (instead of 3).

Table 9

Comparative budgets to show optimum life

	Year	3	4	5
		£	£	£
A. *Old's flow in year*		400	700	1300
B. New's cumulative flow over various potential life-spans:				
At purchase		1750	1750	1750
In 1st year		–	–	–
In 2nd year		200	200	200
In 3rd year		400	400	400
In 4th year			700	700
In 5th year				1300
Scrap receipts		(50)	(50)	(50)
Totals for each life-span		2300	3000	4300
C. *New's average per year* of life				
(= notional rent)		767	750	860

Revised asset values

Old's owner must feel pleased that he bought when he did. Ownership now confers enhanced benefits, in the sense of obviating need to pay the extra for a dearer New.

"Every valuation is a comparison"; the gratifying contrast with New raises Old's deprival value. The original and revised values can be shown in diagram form.

Life is here extended from OK to OM. The value pattern, originally expected to be CK′K, is revised at E (end of year 2) and becomes CFHM′M.

The value can be found with HAVE and HAVE NOT budgets, as in Table 10 below. Their figures are the same as in Table 4 till the price rise late in year 2. The post-change columns, on the right, thereafter put New's rent

Diagram 11 **Revaluation after specific price-change**

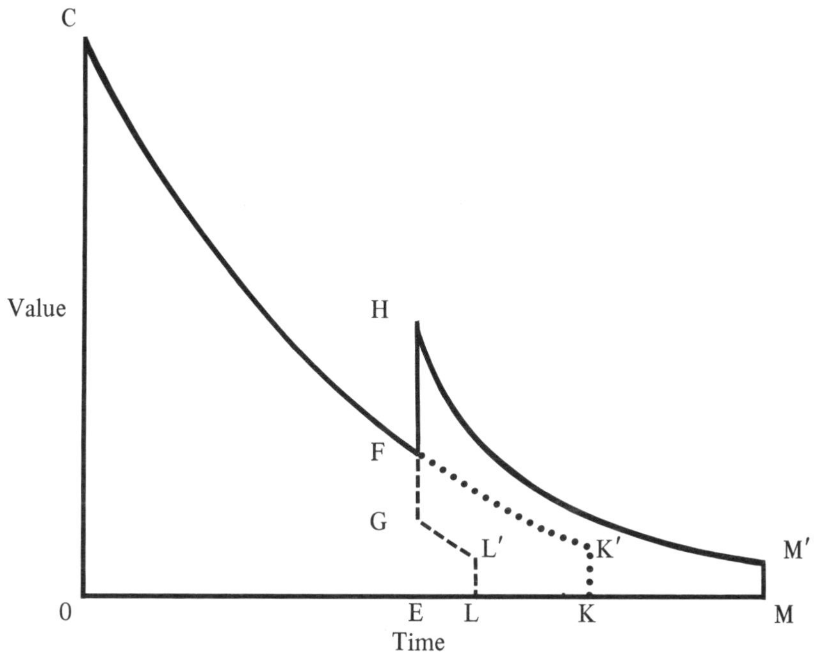

at its increased level of £750. Thus they lift the yearly benefits of ownership in line *iii*, and the values in line *iv* (*eg*, at the end of year 2, future yearly benefits will be £(350 + 50 + 50) = £450, and so value jumps from £250 to £450).

"Replacement cost" is not replacement price"

Comparison of Tables 7 and 10 (pages 45 and 51) shows that specific price-change upsets value patterns more than does general change. Not only has specific change stretched Old's life, but it has (partly because of this extra spell of service) raised Old's value disproportionately: the price jump of 40% has raised value by 80% (from £250 to £450 – see page 51, last line of table, year 2 values). Remember that the HAVE and HAVE NOT budgets must allow for the new life and repair figures as well as the new price, and so the final line may well change more or less than price. As page 14 pointed out, "replacement cost" covers more than "replacement price".

Table 10

Revaluation after specific price-change

Year of life	0	1	2		3	4	4
			Pre-	*Post-*			
	£	£	£	£	£	£	£
HAVE budget							
Old's cash flows	1250		200		400	700	(50)
HAVE NOT budget							
New's notional rent		600	600		750	750	
Net benefit of owning for year		600	400		350	50	50
Deprival value							
–future years' benefits, as foreseen:							
Prior to inflation (line iii, page 36)	1250	650	250				
After inflation (line iii, above)				450	100	50	

An unfortunate and little recognised consequence is that the short-cut of revaluation with a specific index may yield inaccurate results. Published indices presumably reflect the prices of brand-new assets. The accountant needs other indices as well, to reflect values of worn assets.

The revised balance sheet after specific change

In the balance sheet, the primary asset's gross and net values must be raised as in Table 11, which shows the figures for our example at the end of year 2. The price of a new asset is £1,750; Table 10 puts current value (worn) at £450: so depreciation must be the difference of £1,300. The net increase of £200 is reflected in the equity.

If (as is probable) the secondary assets are unlike the primary asset, they may not appreciate at the same pace. Then they will no longer match cumulative depreciation. A shortfall will clearly create problems if the asset is to be replaced at the end of its life.

Table 11

Balance sheet, end of year 2, revalued after specific price-change

	(1) *Pre-revaluation* £	(2) *Post-revaluation* £
Primary asset (new)	1250	1750
less Cumulative depreciation	1000	1300
Net value (worn)	250	450
Secondary assets	1000	1000
	1250	1450
Capital	1250	1250
Revaluation surplus		
Primary asset		200
	1250	1450

Annual charges

Specific price-change alters depreciation charges of later years. For instance, Tables 4 and 10 show them going up to £350 (from £200) in year 3, and to £50 (from nil) in year 4. In the end, the cumulative total will mount (see line *iii* of Table 10) to £600 + £400 + £350 + £50 + £50 = £1450. This is more than the original investment (£1250), but less than replacement price (£1750).

So should the later charges to the income statement be less than depreciation cost, or equal to it, or (backlog again) more than it? Your answer to this question depends (see page 12) on how you define the owner's "well-offness", *ie*, on what sort of capital is to be maintained.

The capital maintenance test

You must choose between three possibilities:

(1) Money capital.

(2) Real capital.

In the absence of general price-change, (1) and (2) are the same.

If the owner ends up with assets worth £1,250, he is as well-off as when he started – in the important sense of still being able to buy much the same basket of goods-in-general and so keep up his living standard.

(3) Physical capital (or "operating capacity")

If the owner ends up with less than £1750, he is less well-off in the sense of ability to replace the given asset.

You therefore face the difficult choice between real and physical capital. Accountants are split on the question. I favour real capital[1] because (*a*) the main reason for measuring income is to give the owner a guide to his consumption plans; (*b*) the calculations can go wildly astray if they hinge on physical rather than economic characteristics; and (*c*) replacements can be quite different from the first asset, because of technical improvements, etc.

Entries in the income statement

If *real* capital is chosen as yardstick, the depreciation provisions must maintain the owner's command over goods-in-general, not ability to replace the given asset. The low charges of the original estimate remain correct for the whole life, since they here keep the owner's wealth at its starting level. Thus, in our example, the year 3 charge is still only £200 (as on page 36); if revenue is say £800, profit is £600, as in column (1) of Table 12.

But the same profit can be reached by a route that is more informative, and fits in with current values in the balance sheet. Column (2) shows this alternative. It charges the current (*ie*, higher) depreciation (here £350 – see page 51); but then it credits the appreciation on the slice of asset realised in the year (£150 – the difference between the current and historical charges of £350 and £200). Profit is again £600.

If the firm wants to maintain its assets at their expanded level of £1750, it may finance this £500 addition by for instance making voluntary appropriations of profit, say at £250 each year (see the foot of columns (1) and (2)).

1 I argue the case more fully in *Accounting Values and Inflation* (McGraw-Hill, London 1975), chapter 8.

Table 12

Alternative forms of income statement, for year 3, after specific price change

Type of capital to be maintained	(1) *Real*	(2) *Real*	(3) *Physical*
	£	£	£
Revenue			
Trading	800	800	800
Realised appreciation (current less historical depreciation, as below)		150	
		950	
Less Depreciation			
Historical cost (page 36)	200		
Current cost (page 51)		350	350
Backlog (see below)			300
			650
Profit	600	600	150
Less Appropriation for increase in specific cost, say	250	250	
	350	350	

If the vote goes to *physical* capital, then the higher depreciation figures of the post-change estimate (page 51) are again charged, as in column (3), but the income statement fails to recognise the appreciation. And, to make good the seeming under-provision at revaluation date, backlog depreciation may be charged too (in our example, say £300 in year 3). One can imagine cases in which this double burden would be intolerable.

Fall in value

In the absence of general price change, the values of depreciating assets are perhaps more likely to need downward than upward revaluation. There are depressing forces in plenty, *eg*, accidents and unexpected physical faults, or economic change such as drop in demand for the asset's product or the invention of a better model.

These forces will tend to lessen Old's life as well as its value. The figures can be found from tables analogous to 9 and 10. The value curve may take a new shape such as CFGL′L in Diagram 11 (*ie*, the asset will be scrapped at L instead of K); or, if the depressing forces are strong enough, value will plunge vertically to the scrap figure, and the asset will be sold at E.

(C) COMBINED GENERAL AND SPECIFIC PRICE-CHANGE

Now that we have seen how general and specific changes affect accounting when they come separately, we can more readily understand what happens when – as is usual – they come hand-in-hand.

A table of HAVE and HAVE NOT budgets, on the same lines as earlier tables, will show the new patterns of value and depreciation cost. The asset's optimum life may change, thanks to the specific ingredient.

Real *versus* physical capacity

Once again one must choose between the three concepts of capital maintenance (page 52). A switch to almost any form of inflation accounting means rejection of money capital. To my mind, real capital still commands respect, while the faults of physical capital become even more plain.

Apart from its other virtues, the real capital concept turns a spotlight onto an important quantity – *real gain or loss* (*ie*, the surplus or shortfall between a specific value and what the value would have been if it had moved like prices-in-general). Suppose an asset cost £100 when the general and specific indices stood at 100; if thereafter they rise to 140 and 150 respectively, the owner has made a real gain ("real holding gain" or "real appreciation") of £10. This figure seems an eminently sensible measure of his increase in "well-offness".

The "Inflation Accounting Standard"

Despite the arguments for real capital, SSAP 16 (the Standard dealing with inflation accounting, issued in 1980) opts for "Current Cost Accounting", *ie*, the physical basis. Thus it prescribes a CCA income statement that includes an adjustment to raise historical depreciation to the level of current replacement cost.

Admittedly the physical concept is often the easier to apply. Its entries are the crude ones described in section B above. Its advocates argue that, if the owner is enabled to replace his physical capital, he can turn a blind eye to inflation: specific prices are a good enough surrogate for costs raised with the general index, so there is no call for further refinement. This is sensible where specific and general prices move in close step, but can have bad results when they diverge. Suppose new inventions make a firm's machinery almost worthless; current cost depreciation will then dive, leaving profit at a cheerful figure that fails to reflect the disaster; historical charges, raised with the general index, yield a profit that here is vastly more prudent.

The "ideal" system

If accounting is to be reformed thoroughly, there are strong grounds for measuring income by the test of real capital. But there are also strong grounds for using current values for assets and costs. The advocate of real capital can get the best of both worlds by blending the two concepts, *ie*, by using the so-called "ideal" (or hybrid) system.[1]

This values assets at current levels. But it analyses their appreciation into its two components:

(*a*) Fictitious, *ie*, inflation induced. This part is found by applying a general index factor to historical cost.

(*b*) Real, *ie*, the residue (sometimes negative).

It shows the two figures separately in the equity. (*a*) is given some such name as "inflation allowance" and is left permanently (unless the general index moves down again). (*b*) is called "unrealised real appreciation"; later, if it is realised, it is credited to income (following the same logic as column (2) on page 54). The final income figures is thus geared to real capital.

Example

Illustrative figures may be helpful. Suppose a firm starts the year with £1,000 in cash, and at once invests this in a machine – when both general and special indices stand at 100. Very soon after, the indices jump to 140 and 150 respectively, and then stay steady.

[1] The name was given on page 45 of the *Background Papers* to Exposure Draft 18, Current Cost Accounting, published in 1976 by the Accounting Standards Committee.

At the time of this price change, reformed accounts will write up the asset from £1,000 to £1,500, and add the £500 appreciation to equity. The ideal system unravels the components of the £500; the fictional gain of £400 (= $\frac{40}{50}$ x £500), duly ascribed to inflation; and the £100 residue – real appreciation, classed as a type of profit. So the balance sheet shows equity as:

	£
Capital	1 000
Capital – inflation adjustment	400
Unrealised real appreciation	100
	1 500

Suppose next that the machine is thereafter hired out for a yearly rent of £350; and that historical depreciation cost per year is one-fifth of the asset's price, *ie*, £200. In the ordinary accounts – see column (1) of table 13 – profit for the ensuing year is thus £350 – £200 = £150.

It is less, as inflation accounting demands, in the two brands of reformed statements illustrated in columns (2) and (3). These raise depreciation to current cost: one-fifth of the asset's new value of £1,500 is £300, so the charge goes up to this realistic figure. By the physical test of column (3), profit is cut to only £50.

But the ideal system does not overlook the £100 of real gain shown above. It now deems one-fifth of this gain ($\frac{1}{5}$ x £100 = £20) to have been realised by the year's operation, and transfers this £20 to revenue as in column (2). The resulting profit is £70. It meets the test of real capital maintenance: £350, less the £200 historical depreciation raised with the general index to £280, is likewise £70.

Thus the ideal system gives up-to-date values and charges, but also a profit that satisfies the logic of real capital maintenance.

Unfortunately, none of the proposed reform methods will be easy to explain to laymen. Inflation's effects are not simple: and, if accounts are to respond adequately, they cannot be simple either.

Table 13

Final accounts – alternative versions after revaluation

	1	2	3
Type of capital to be maintained	*Money*	*Real* ("ideal system")	*Physical*
	£	£	£
Income statement			
Revenue			
Rent	350	350	350
Realised appreciation		20	
		370	
Less Depreciation			
Historical	200		
Current cost		300	300
Profit	150	70	50
Balance sheet			
Fixed asset (new)	1000	1500	
Less Depreciation	200	300	as (2)
	800	1200	
Secondary assets	350	350	
	1150	1550	
Capital	1000	1000	1000
Inflation adjustment		400	
Revaluation surplus			500
Unrealised real appreciation (100–20)		80	
Profit	150	70	50
	1150	1550	1550

Conclusion

These five chapters have tried to spell out the life story of a depreciating asset. They have shown how a wide set of cash flows controls optimum life and asset value. They have argued that we should deem asset values to govern depreciation charges (and not the other way round). They have described the traditional methods of depreciation as handy but crude, and explained how to test their adequacy in a given case with the budgets of deprival value. These budgets enable us also to evolve more sensitive methods that will allow – where the need arises – for complex cash patterns, cost-of-capital, inflation, and current values.

The next few years will see great changes in accounting. We must hope that depreciation methods can develop in ways that satisfy both reason and practical needs.

6 Index